Faraway Tables
poems

Yorkshire Publishing
TULSA

ISBN: 978-1-960810-54-0
Faraway Tables

Cover image credit: "Faraway Tables," original 16" x 20"
painting by Gene McCormick, acrylic on canvas.

For permission requests, write to the publisher at the address below.

Yorkshire Publishing
1425 E 41st Pl
Tulsa, OK 74105
www.YorkshirePublishing.com
918.394.2665

Printed in Canada.

Faraway Tables

poems

eric d. goodman

Also by Eric D. Goodman

Wrecks and Ruins
The Color of Jadeite
Setting the Family Free
Womb: a novel in utero
Tracks: A Novel in Stories
Flightless Goose

Learn more about Eric D. Goodman and his
work at www.EricDGoodman.com

For Shirley J. Brewer,
poet, mixologist, friend.

Contents

Instruction Manual

Taste it—
fruit from a native land,
a melon or succulent, unfamiliar.

Risk disappointment;
anticipate delight.

Use caution:
open yourself
to the possibility
of wonder.

I.

Savor

Patience

Sleep still heavy upon you,
you ask me to do it. I want it as badly as you do.

Through the morning fog, I find the bag,
pulverize dark beans into powder,
press dust into metal cup,
stumble through the morning routine.

We wait, listen, anticipate,
place two mugs upon the granite counter,
desperate for delivery. We wait.

Outside the kitchen window,
milky mist rolls along marshy grounds.

You ask how much longer, although you know
there's no rushing such things.

A steamy aroma rises and teases us,
promises we will be blessed for effort and patience.

And yet, what patience? what effort?
Certainly not our own.

These beans have traveled across four years,
across the globe from Indonesia to our home:

planted, matured, harvested—
dried, milled, tested—
roasted, packaged, shipped—

and what do you or I know of this journey
besides the purchased reward of indulgence,

erupting now, at this moment, as I fill our cups
we take our sips, awaken,
and are raptured into a new day.

COVID-19

—20
—21
—22
—23

You wanted what any of us wants:
to survive.

Unable to kill you,
only to keep you down,

demoted from book title
to just another

peripheral poem.

Notre Dame Bardo

In this sacred fortress,
one of fifty thousand churches in France,
sunlight filters through stained glass.

Serrated red erupts from the window,
warms the cold stone floor,
spills over your white shirt.

Passion and fury,
life and death,
pulsate in a hum of energy.

The soles of your hiking shoes lift
in this Bardo
between one reality and the next.

An inferno infects,
warms, radiates
through you, through this place.

In this disorienting moment:
recklessness ... clarity ...
connected to everything and nothing at once.

Toast to Friendship

Seeing my children stand there
in Kiev's Independence Square,
beneath the victory column—
Slavic goddess and protector of home
presiding with branch in hand—

I remembered my visit decades earlier
to Russia, as a student,
just after the Iron Curtain fell.

How peaceful a place the world
seemed finally to be:
young Russians and Ukrainians,
Americans and Brits,
toasting to international friendship
with shots of Stolichnaya and Jim Beam,
chased by strong-smelling black bread.

Decades later, as my children looked up
at the obelisk in this independent nation,
it seemed, at the moment, that peace had endured.

Within a year, the square had become a burning battleground,
The Revolution of Dignity taking a hundred lives.

These people in Kiev—people just like us—
no longer worried about
when to go to the store for toothpaste,
but whether their sons and daughters
would live in an independent nation,
or live at all.

And now, this special military operation
(shall we call it a war?)
threatens civilian life
in cities and communities just like ours.

Buildings blown open,
communities torn apart,
refugees seeking asylum.

When this passes,
let my adult children stand
in Independence Square again
alongside the children
of my Ukrainian and Russian friends
and let the new generation toast
to international friendship
just as we did, so sincerely, not so long ago.

Snowless

We prayed for a mild winter
after last year's blizzards

and were answered with
a sadly snowless season,

biting cold and wet,
lonely shovel left in the shed.

Spring arrives, but
you wouldn't know it:

short days, long nights,
harsh wind and gray skies.

Flowers struggle to bud,
submit to smothering frost.

The world outside too damp for a fire pit,
we huddle around the glow of the television,

which offers brighter scenes
than those beyond the window:

cold, hard ground, yellow grass,
tree branches reaching for a rare touch of sun.

Torrential rain loosens the mud,
and the worms celebrate.

The birds arrive,
but how can we enjoy their songs

about the frenzy of feasting
on the misery of worms?

We're no fools,
we can read the markings in the dirt:

snowless winter and
muddy spring announce

a miserably humid summer
followed by autumn—

our favorite season,
the one that rings in

the death and decay,
of another winter,

this one, perhaps,
with a healthy snowfall.

Relics

The two of us amble through
Baltimore's Museum of Industry,
our footsteps echoing off antique machinery.

Some forty years ago we came here as children,
curious hands sticky with candy and cola,
as we ran from the cannery to communications,
never imagining ourselves still in touch—
or alive, for that matter—
as older men.

Reconnecting on social media,
we consider this venue of our elementary school field trip
an ideal location for coming together.

The relics around us boast of yesterday's Baltimore,
a thriving center of industry;
our conversation turns from shared childhood memories
to the day-to-day strangers we've become.

As we explore the origins of the old oyster cannery,
we consider our rekindled friendship food for thought.

Decades may have passed between us,
but our bond remains durable,
like these vestiges of a bygone age.

We consider the divergent occurrences in our lives
as we glance at the vintage printing press,
a demonstration sharing with us
how easily the movable letters connect,
disconnect, reconnect.

What Time Is It?

The mantle clock requires winding.
I take the key and turn it like an old animatronic.
Good for 30 days.

In the parlor, grandfather's
brass pendulum hangs still.
I crank up the three weights
so the ticks, tocks, and Westminster chimes
will continue for a week.

The living room's cuckoo clock is silent,
the bird peeking out of the open door, mid-song.
With a pull of the first chain, then the second,
the heavy metal pinecones rise,
giving voice to the cuckoo
who finishes her song.

"We need a timekeeper to keep track
of when to wind the clocks,"
I say, and my smart speaker
tells me the time.

As for the Ticket

Don't burn the tongue
on flavor still too hot.

Eat slowly,
savor the sustenance
that will certainly end too soon.

The dinner is delicious,
the main course, half-devoured,
still piping.

As for the ticket, no, not yet.
Keep it at bay.

No need to rush the bill
that nobody wants to pay.

These passionate days
steeped in desire and warmth and bliss
do not come for free.

The laughter and clinking glasses,
clanking cutlery and riveting conversation
at a table of friends with so much to say
that half the fresh ideas fall
like forgotten crumbs for the less fortunate
scavenging the cracks between the floorboards.

The bill always comes at the end.

The thing to do is to avoid eye contact
with the waiter standing by in his black tuxedo,
lurking slyly in the shadows,
silver platter in white-gloved hand,
in search of an entry point;

not to look into the mirror at the aging stranger there
as you visit the restroom more frequently
than you used to;

not to spend too much time sharing recent
photographs of the kids and family,
only to realize that the photos you are showing
are ten, fifteen, twenty years old.

The thing to do is to pace yourself,
chew your food until the flavor is spent,
take your time, sip and savor
the wine and beer and scotch and cognac
that you once gulped
with a greedy thirst,
and don't be afraid to add a little ice
or water if that will make the flavor linger.

If you can choose the tastiest morsels,
the finest beverages, optimal companionship,
stretch out your servings so that
you don't outpace your hunger
and end up uncomfortably full,
perhaps—just perhaps—
you will make the most
of the restaurant's operating hours
and the bill will not arrive
until you are ready to receive it.

Embracing Hermithood

The hair is the first to grow.
The salt-and-pepper business cut
filling out into a lion's mane,
gushing down the head and over the shoulders
like a SWAT team's rappelling ropes over a fortress
during the raid on an out-of-control dictator
threatening our nation.

Then the facial hair,
from stubble to beard to lumberjack
to mountain man,
the picture completing when cooler weather rests
unbuttoned flannel over T-shirts
and introduces fire pits for poking.

No need to phone it in
when an IM or email will do.
Work becomes remote,
audio calls and screen sharing
the new team huddle.

No necessity to go out, no reason to drive,
hermit life made not only bearable—
embraceable.

The need to appear disappears.

The pandemic drives us into
our isolated caves. Gives us an excuse
to be what we want to be.

Down

It's easy to understand the bat,
this creature of the night
who hangs upside down for relaxation.

How it feels to have no lift,
only able to
            fall
                  into flight,

everything
           down,
                beginning with descent,

never an opportunity to jump,
to ascend into flight
unless already
                falling,

blindly searching for a higher place,
forever pulled down
                      by
                          gravity.

Yin Yang Yankee Doodle

When I looked back at my calendar,
the day I celebrated my promotion was
the day you received your cancer diagnosis.

I found myself reconsidering that old,
thrown-off notion of
"balance in the universe,"
some spiritual Robin-Hood force that seizes
from "here" to bequeath "there,"
instigating pain someplace
to confer pleasure someplace else;

the great balancing force that allows
the U S of A to reap so many benefits,
soak in ocean hot tubs of wealth and comfort,
wield influence over the world,
a benevolent bully.

Today,
people are dying and being born,
are becoming ill and becoming well,
getting married and divorced,
falling in and out of love,
feeling pleasure and pain.

Mask are being worn like commemorative medals,
other masks are thrown aside like burdensome shackles,
knees being taken and hearts being covered.

Hearts are being repaired and replaced
and broken and swollen
with love and disease.

Still unaware of your unrevealed diagnosis,
I remember I felt on top of the world
after that unanticipated promotion

until a rejection letter for my latest novel arrived to
remind me that all news was not good news.

The manuscript did not meet their needs at that time,
needs apparently met by someone else,
someone undoubtably celebrating the abundance
of good fortune befalling them,
perhaps unaware, perhaps fully aware
that the cost of their success
was another writer considering giving up.

One day after receiving the rejection letter,
I saw you and your new scar,
and learned that, in a matter of a few short weeks,
you'd been diagnosed with cancer and cured.

I discovered that the day of your diagnosis
matched the day of my good fortune;
the day of your cure matched the day of my rejection.

Balance.

Fire Pit Season

A squirrel considers a nut,
then opts for a softer acorn
and carries it up a Nordic pine.

The bunnies vacationing
in the woodpile return
to their underground den.

Twin foxes on patrol
circle the yard a second time.

Deer approach the dogwood trees
to sample the meaty red berries.

Buzzards coast rings overhead
as an injured groundhog
takes shelter beneath a foundation.

Neighborhood dogs consult one another,
their barks echoing
off the remaining foliage.

Brown leaves gently freckle,
the paling green yard.

Crows caw in the branches,
while geese migrate arrowheads above.

Cooler weather announces itself
as a returning guest on our threshold,
ready to warm itself by the fire.

Newsworthy

The death toll: staggering—
wildfires in the west, hurricanes in the east,

civil unrest breaking out in the sandy, faraway republic
bursting with old Soviet warheads.

Headlines astound television viewers
and social media scrollers alike—

The same day one person is abducted
another, from last week, found mutilated in a ditch.

An atypical news day taking eyeballs
off presidential gaffes and congressional squabbling.

The fatal electrical fire at the puppy mill outdone
only by the deadly gas leak at the orphanage.

Somehow lost in this news cycle:
The press release announcing my book's publication day.

Red Hat

The long white beard
I allowed to stake claim on my face

gave me the courage to don
the red suit and hat,

forgetting myself,
becoming someone else.

At the city's drive-thru holiday light show,
I mounted the plywood sleigh.

Waving at the children in each car with a "ho-ho-ho,"
calling witticisms to parents,

the joy expressed by their laughter and smiles paled
next to the feeling of warmth within my coat.

To experience this greatness,
I had only to let go of myself.

The Web in Your Path

As you walk along the trail
and your face meets a spider's web,
resist the instinct to swipe at it with a stick,
or force your way through.

Consider the work that has gone into it.
Not only the hours of hard labor—
frantic spinning of thread throughout the night—
but the artistry.

How would you feel if some animal
larger than you came tromping through your yard
and bumped into your home, took out
a window or busted through a corner?

What if this large animal—a bear,
perhaps a giant—
became irritated by your irrelevant shack
and thrashed about, demolishing
your roof, your secure home, tearing it
down to its foundation?

Think of how hard you worked to create
this safe place for your family—
this home where you can eat and rest,
snuggle with your loved ones,
maybe play a board game or watch a movie.

When you encounter the web in your path,
step calmly back, gently duck under the thread,
and walk on.

II.

Ache

Renovate

Under the weight of history's suppressing precedent,
the echo of agony lingers, throbs.

A resounding plea bleeds from society's extremities
for justice's embers to ignite and illuminate.

In these renamed streets of fallen monuments
to mis-honored traitors,
cries fill the air like birdsong:
"I can't breathe!" resonates,
a look back at injustice, a look forward to reconciliation.

United believers tinker
with the authority of systemic shackles.

Spirits aflame with resilient fury,
ordinary folk strive for the extraordinary,
bartering injustice for justice,
outrage for opportunity.

Like orthodox icons, unsuspecting martyrs
inhabit banners and posters and murals,
beacons recognized by the world
as we say their names.

In these cities and towns, inequality festers
beneath an ancient infrastructure
that is difficult to extricate,
embedded as it is in society's foundations.

Facing the skyscrapers and heavy ivory towers,
burning from somewhere deep within comes a bellow
to stoke the embers, burn it down,
to dismantle and rebuild.

No one truly knows the fit and feel
of the other's shoe.

In this evolving waltz toward progress,
let us kick off our shoes,
stride with open arches,
guided by ferocity and compassion,
toward a glimmering new horizon.

Pandemerick

We put 2020 to bed,
"Next year will be better," we said.
But on further inspection—
—COVID spread! Insurrection!
A worse year may yet be ahead.

Sisson's

At Sisson's,
the bar of dark, polished wood
invites elbows and forearms to rest.

The mirrored wall,
obstructed by half-emptied bottles—
Jack, Jim, Jose, Hennessey—
allows you to see behind you
as people enter and assess,
take a seat and order a drink:

the booth of youngsters being carded
and asked politely to leave,
lowering their heads in shame as they
scuffle out to look for a more easygoing
watering hole;

the table of workers from Cross Street Market
discussing plans for the weekend ahead,
glad to be through another week of
slinging shrimp cocktails,
icing wide-eyed fish,
frosting bakery cupcakes,
selling buckets of flowers and
bushels of crabs and
sandwiches stacked high with pastrami;

the tall table of ladies in tight dresses and skirts
with metallic-green-shadowed eyes that roam
as though in search of something looking back at them.

To your left, a street musician and a performance artist
exchange theories about the redemption
of the human race and make plans
for how we will come together
to save the world from ourselves.

On your right, a young man is talking
about the five novels he has written,
not one of them published,
as though in search of a piano man
to sing him a song.

An Indian physician consoles him,
explains that publication is not what matters,
that leaving a mark on the universe is what counts,
and the writing of a book, singing of a song, or touching of a life
is the true measure.

"But Doc," the street musician calls over,
overhearing him in the pause of their
save-the-world discussion,
"Does a tree make a sound if no one is around to hear it?"

"The universe hears it," the physician replies,
taking a sip of his scotch on the rocks.

You look from the musician on your left
to the doctor on your right
and offer a smile, raise your glass,
and take a drink.

The smile is contagious. Not overdone,
not a smug smirk, just
an upspoken solidarity.

For a moment, a shared earnestness hovers
where smoke once lingered,
a smile on each face—
doctor, writer, musician, artist, you.

And me?
I'm sitting at the corner of the bar,
under the video game poker screen that no one is playing,
watching you without aid of a mirror,
content to be in this small and insignificant
pocket of the cosmos.

Of the Castle

Your armor was dull, tarnished,
long before you hung it up,
traded it in for a worn tee-shirt
and outdated joggers.

But kneel before me just the same,
a knight before his queen.

You, with your strength and solidity,
are not my fortress,
as you once imagined,

but a pedestal
to showcase my eminence.

Don't expect me to roar,
but you might earn a purr
if you greet me with a corsage,
open the door before me,

remind me of the one pleasant sensation
from an unkind history

when I pretended
to enjoy being a vassal
knowing all along I was your liege.

Control

When my computer's platform
for virtual meetings crashed,
and my IT specialist recommended I give over control,
I eagerly abdicated.

Cursor moved as though on autopilot,
clicked here and there,
scanned code that made no sense to me.

How easy it would be to relinquish control
to someone who knew better
how to navigate the mysterious code of life—

but before I could explore the fantasy,
IT had returned control to me

just in time for my next virtual meeting.

Celebratory Condolence

Sometimes I worry
that I might say the wrong thing
on a sympathy card,
or birthday card,

or worse, that I might
mix up the cards:

my over-the-hill, fifty-year-old friend receiving
"I know this is a difficult time for you,
but you will get through this,"

while my mourning colleague, fingertips damp
from corralling tears, reads,

"Celebrate this day! Now begins the exciting
next chapter in your life. The best days
are yet to come!"

Perhaps "thinking of you" is the safest phrase,
whether offering congratulation or condolence,
followed by "thoughts and prayers"
and an affectionate signature.

Sassy

The sky's pink hue tells me it is nearly 5:40,
time for your morning walk.
I reach for your leash.

You've been prancing through my mind
these hollow morning hours.

Why am I surprised

when I don't hear the clicking of your nails
upon the hardwood,

don't see your excited stretch
at the sound of the leash,

you wagging as I still your bean-curled twirl
to find the loop of your blue collar?

I see your collar on the table.

How I always wanted to sleep in
an extra ten minutes
when it was my turn to walk you.

How I long to walk with you—
at any hour—now.

Barefoot

The girl with hunger in her eyes
wants to scream,
to brush the glitter of her hometown from her stilettos,
and cartwheel to freedom.

Her sense of not belonging in the city's pulse:
a secret so dark and deep
it can never be shared,
(though everyone close to her
can perceive it).

He takes her hand,
leads her to his car,
coerces her away from the city's disco and dazzle
to the barefoot world she thinks she wants

where the only sound is the wind,
the only shimmer comes from stars,
the only dance music
is the beating of his heart next to hers.

True

One may think

nonfiction writers
tell the truth
with dates and facts,

fiction writers hide
themselves behind
characters and MacGuffins,

while poets use smoke and mirrors
or a sleight of hand
to conjure emotion.

But could it be

the poet who
exposes the soul,

the fiction writer who
reveals what is true

while the nonfiction writer hides
behind undisputable facts?

Avocado Toast

The waitress waits.

"Avocado toast," you decide,
doing the right thing,
remaining reliably plant-based,
supporting farmers.

Then you frown at me and ask,
"Twenty-three dollars for avocado toast, really?"

not knowing the real value
of an Avocado from Mexico,
of Tancitaro farmers—large and small—

of Los Zetas,
La Familia Michoacana,
The Knights Templar,
The Auto Defensas,

of skimming, extortion, bribes,
family kidnappings,
borrowing ransom money
that can never be paid back,

of burning warehouses,
murder, control,

of 18 gallons of water
taken from residents,
from small farmers
who can no longer grow
their personal crops,

who depend on delivery trucks
for drinking water
that once came from their environment—

of violence and death and fighting back—

of homes and vehicles riddled with bullets,
dead bodies on dusty roads,

of a child's stilled heart
no bigger than an avocado seed.

Social Media Boycott

A pity,
to pass through the lingering days of a year,
long, cold winters,
flash-in-the-pan summers,
occasional whiffs of spring flowers
and leaps into crispy piles of autumn leaves,

the whole year waiting for that brilliant moment:
the accumulation of "happy birthday" greetings
on your electronic wall for all to see.

Passionate copy-and-paste words of heartfelt feeling—
"happy birthday" and "have a good one"—
heartfelt gifs and images and emojis
evoking laughter or tears.

Humanity joining in birthday wishes
like so many cards that were not worth the posting.

Oh, you can relate to the reason behind the boycott:
the overreach of the venue,
injustice of the situation,
mistreatment,
wrongs in need of righting.

You stand with the boycotters in solidarity!
We will not take this, we will disappear
from this electronic venue to inflict
the sting of our strike!
We will be missed!

But did it have to happen on my birthday?
you wonder as you find solace
in your social media "memories"
from this day in yesteryears.

Fado

I.

It's been six months since Portugal,
and yet, we find ourselves listening still
to the soft, acoustic sounds
of traditional Portuguese music.

From the melancholy notes of fado
that vibrate inside us,
to the lightness of guitarra,
tickling the bones,

the playlist as addictive
as the egg custards and strong coffee
we consumed daily, like vitamins.

II.

Thrilled by Scottish bagpipers
on a misty gray day at Edinburgh Castle
as they serenaded us in plaid kilts,

the souvenir CD of the Royal Scots Dragoon Guard
does not carry the same excitement,
even coupled with a hand-delivered
Glenfiddich or two.

Instead, the recorded bagpipes
playing *Amazing Grace*
bring to mind a memorial procession
marching along the cobblestoned Royal Mile,
or a police funeral in Chicago.

III.

Boisterous oompah music
in the beer halls of Munich—
Augustiner and Hofbrauhaus—
matched the lively crowds of revelers
raising their steins
at long, communal tables of scuffed wood.

The music and beer,
smiling faces and clinking mugs
made the accordion, trumpets, tuba, trombones
all part of the delicious froth.

The same music piped in
from a home speaker works well
for a dinner of bratwurst and sauerkraut,
but does not evoke the joy
of those faraway tables.

VI.

This afternoon, we bathe
in the *Waters of March*,
translating some Portuguese lyrics
allowing others to flow by on sound alone.

We dry ourselves beneath the warm breath of fado:
guitarra and viola,
a woman wailing,
craving what she once embraced tightly
but now misses so much that it aches.

Backyard Weeds

Watching the documentary
about the life of plants,

observing how root systems
map out the most efficient paths
to water and nutrients the same way

that our civilization maps
a public transit system—

the visual image of the roots appearing
identical to a large city's subway map—

it occurs to me:

despite our pretension
that humankind is superior
to every other life form—

animal and plant alike—

we are really no more consequential
than the weeds
in our backyard.

Power of Positive Thinking

I'm going to a new home,
where the servers are robots,
and the food is made with compassion.

I'm not afraid,
because I know anything is possible
in this all-inclusive resort.

I'll see my loved ones daily:
the living ones will grudgingly stop by
and the dead are sure to flirt with my daydreams.

Luxurious, adjustable bed,
cable TV, and a cabin companion
for cards, conversation, and laughter.

Gourmet meals,
unlimited snacks and drinks,
and the recreation area drenched in sunlight.

In our new palace, rules don't matter,
and the only thing that counts is an appreciation
for warm, fuzzy moments gone by.

I'll make myself happy there,
in the land of the living dead,
my Hospice.

Water Fall Blues

I've got the water fall blues, little dewdrop,
yeah, those thirsty, dry-mouthed water fall blues.

I.

As the decades-long drought drags on,
Lake Powell's bright white
bathtub ring stretches
and waters evaporate.

Lake Mead reveals secrets:
a body in a barrel, bones washed up on the shore,
a wrecked B-29 bomber,
prehistoric salt mines,
an entire ghost town, homes for the freshly
discovered human remains that likely migrated from
early days of a mafia-run Vegas.

Damn, Hoover.

II.

In the dusty lands of the Navajo Nation,
a native squeezes the final drops of water
from a plastic jug, wondering
when the next delivery truck will arrive
from the white lands surrounding.

Not enough water in Italy's River Po
to contain the WWII-era German tanks or cargo ships,
not enough water remaining to allow cargo ships of today
to bring necessities for those depending on
the river.

In Rome, the River Tiber opens its waters to reveal
a bridge built during Emperor Nero's rule. Is this
the "Bridge to the Twenty-First Century" I heard
tell of twenty years ago?

On the Spanish-Portuguese border,
the abandoned town of Aceredo
has returned to the surface
as the Alto Lindoso Reservoir fades away.

III.

Along Spain's Iberian Peninsula,
the Dolmen of Guadelperal exposes itself,
a stone circle from 5,000 BC,
affectionately known as Spanish Stonehenge.

In Serbia, a Nazi warship peeks
out of the Danube, then another,
then a fleet entire.

Along Germany's Rhine, hunger stones
from yesteryears—1947, 1959, 2003, 2018—
issue a warning of the scarcity to come.

Iraq's drying Mosul Dam Reservoir brings to light
an entire city from the Bronze Age,
a 3,400-year-old gem from the Mitanni Empire.

IV.

As China's Yangtze recedes, an entire
island emerges, complete with ancient
statues carved from stone.

Park visitors in the United Kingdom's
Crystal City can walk along the dried
lakebed and spy old dinosaur sculptures,
fish out of water.

In Texas, receding waters
reveal fossilized dinosaur tracks,
preserved for 113 million years.

V.

The necessity of water is so real you can taste it,
but there's no denying the beauty of natural wonders
unveiled, the marvel of ancient discoveries reclaimed
from beneath the surface of falling waterlines.

And yet, people are thirsty for water, not discoveries.
The Sinagua and Navajo would drown the mafia victims again,
the dinosaur tracks, ghost towns—even the wonders—
for running water, still water, delivered water.
Any water.

VI.

Driving a rented Skoda, you and I visit
the national park we remember from our last
visit to Croatia, and we find that our off-the-beaten-path
waterfall is nowhere to be found. Has it
evaporated, or can we simply not find it?

A personal loss, worthy of
your tears.

III.

Enough

Immersion

The woman dips her toe into the bath,
into the 120-degree water,
holds it there for a matter of seconds.

Instinct overrides determination—
she pulls out,
waiting for the temperature
on the thermometer to subside,
117, 115, 111.

Then, she eases in,
and is reminded of the thermal baths
of Budapest—

those sun-kissed fountains at Szechenyi,
a golden palace of indoor pools
surrounded by a network of exterior baths,

water pouring from decorative spouts
onto her neck and shoulders,
as she watched waist-deep locals play chess
on boards emerging from the surface.

She joined travelers in the whirlpool's current,
circling like a devout pilgrim around Mecca,
then found paradise in the aromatic baths inside.

Across town, in Buda,
the famous baths in Gellert,
outdone only by the obscure ones
recommended by the café barista
next door to her rented flat
in the ruins of Pest.

The interior baths of various temperatures and themes
tempered frigid ice pools with spicy cauldrons
fiercer than the 110-degree water at home,
these extremes made possible
by the gradual increase and decrease
in temperature from pool to pool.

In those baths, she'd tested tolerance
and emerged resilient,
as a sword grows stronger
when taken from the red-hot forge
and plunged into ice-cold water.

Final whirlpool on the rooftop, overlooking the city,
jet streams relaxed the muscles
she'd pushed to their limits.
A reward for endurance.

Now, as she relaxes in the bath at home,
a Liszt rhapsody ricocheting off the tiled walls
massaging her mind,

she thinks of the frog who voluntarily boils
in an easy broth of consolation
unaware that it will kill.

Eyes closed, listening to the trickling piano
from a bathroom speaker,
falling into a steamy respite,
the woman imagines increasing the temperature—
bit by bit—in those Hungarian baths,

imagines it wouldn't be
such a bad way to go.

gulp

here they come,
closing in

where's my key

it's not that

i'm afraid

not that

i fear their punches,
or the cut of their knives

their requests for money
or demands for my wallet

it's not that

i fear looking them in the eyes
and saying

this is how it is
i don't have any change
i only carry my platinum amex

no

it's just that

i don't want to
put down my
big gulp

Drink

Convenient, yes,
this bottled water
during a rushed morning on the go.

No need to find a go-cup
or fill from the tap.

Nestlé does its very best
to do the work for us,
pumping and bottling millions of gallons
of public water per second.

Not so convenient for the communities,
their public waters carried off on trucks,
encapsulated in plastic,
sold for corporate profit,

community members watching their waters dry up,
their ecosystems wobble,
life within it struggling.

Here, where the water in our toilet
is cleaner than drinking water
accessible to much of the world,

we agree to take advantage
of our pure tap water,

to take that extra minute to fill our own cups.

Moments

Those auto-pilot intervals by car and bus and metro,
the daily commute of ten thousand days
cannot hold a candle to the moment

we lit our wedding-day unity candle,
or spent a bright week in St. Petersburg, Russia
during the darkest days of winter.

The daily grind, hours in the office, working
against time on "high-priority" projects
do not carry the weight of the moment

our first child was born,
the two weeks our second child spent in the ICU,
threadbare days set to the beat of pinging bedside monitors.

Mowing the lawn, cleaning the house,
paying the bills, doing the things
that must be done are more easily forgotten than

that instant thirty years ago when the nurse inserted the catheter,
or the moment months later when our eyes first met,
our fingers intertwined, our lips converged.

Twenty minutes of you and I standing side-by-side
on a trolleybus in Nizhniy Novgorod
on our way to Gardenia American Restaurant

occupy more space in the memory
than decades of punching a clock
or tracing and retracing a commute.

How can I pin down moments,
select them, give them weight,
anchor those greatest hits, I wonder

as I rest upon the half-made bed on a Saturday afternoon,
a book in my hands, some easy Chopin floating in the air,
and you at my side, grading papers on your desk of leg,

the golden sun flickering in through the leaves
of tulip poplars swaying in wind
beyond our window.

Just Enough

Pumped-up music on the car stereo
makes the traffic and parking rituals
part of the fun.

Roaming the perimeter
of the Arena in Baltimore,
Merriweather Post Pavilion,
or Wolftrap,
hoping to score
some half-price tickets
from an overambitious scalper
looking to offload.

Lines for $16 beer, $9 water,
even longer waits for the bathrooms.

Nosebleed seats,
the artists below a postage stamp
and I forgot my magnifying glass.

But the mosh pits and energy,
vibration of the bass,
fist pumps and crowd surfing,
being there, part of the scene.

That was me. But not today.
This evening, I'd rather stay in.

The comfort of home:
lights down low, a cozy chair,
Shine a Light, Rattle and Hum,
Get Back, Stop Making Sense
on the television screen,
or a *Last Waltz* on the *Prairie Wind.*
The music turned up just enough.

A scotch within reach,
the bottle just down the hall,
because, after all,
let's put in a little effort.

Dogged Memories

Oh Bratwurst,
I've spent time with you in the rowdy beer halls of Munich,
pierced you with fork and pulled you from a pool of kraut,
dipped you in spiced mustard and washed you down with bitter beer.

Ah, Kielbasa,
there are intimate candlelit moments with you
in the cavernous restaurants of Warsaw,
sweeter than an after-dinner double shot
of pure potato vodka.

And Bangers,
with your inseparable mash,
some Pimm's and gin as lubricant,
lingering in my memory long after
my digestive tract told me to forget you.

But you, my darling Hot Dog—
affectionately known as Oscar by some
and Ball Park Frank by others—
you bring back the fondest memories.

Skewered by stick and held over a backyard firepit,
grilled over a charcoal flame,
served on a bun with relish and mustard and ketchup.

One bite and I'm transported to good times.

Campfire in Big Sur,
Fourth of July community barbeque in Virginia Beach,
baseball game between naval ship crews in Charleston,
American Festival in Sasebo,
friends and family and dogs and cats and laughter and sun,
some potato salad, deviled eggs, and baked beans on the side.

Bratwurst, Kielbasa, Bangers,
you caught my attention,
but I'll always compare you
to my unwavering American Hot Dog.

Stuffed

One
day I
will get
more stuff
to complete
my longing to
fulfill the American
dream. A little house,
bigger one, a car, then two,
queen-sized bed and enough
furniture and closet space to hold
my collection of clothing and shoes.
The guest room and extra den can become
makeshift closets as the master closet overflows.
Two fridges and a deep freeze ensure we will never want.
All the furniture looks all the better with so many collectables,
but it is so much easier to clean and dust without them lingering.
So, I sell them. I challenge myself to wear each article of clothing
in my house (that belongs to me) at least once before putting
on the same thing twice. I cannot. The concert t-shirt I hold
onto no longer fits. There are holes in my favorite, best-
fitting jeans. If I'm not a hat person, why do I have 10
of them? I ask what I need, what I want, and why
I'm holding on to so many things. Goodwill and
Green Dot take the "favorite" positions on my
speed-dial. Grandpa's ancient reel-to-reel
player, Dad's dusty cassette deck,
my CD player are all boxed up.
Old records, CDs, and DVDs,
gadgets and collectables,
dusted off, packed up
and then sent away.
Life has become
less cluttered
with less
stuff.

1994

Nearly thirty years old, the decision memo
reads like one written today—
but takes me back to a time
before I was aware of such concerns:

to the year that burst with excitement and promise,
the year that I studied abroad in Nizhniy Novgorod,
traveled with you to Moscow and St. Petersburg,
to Gorodets and the Golden Circle,

the year that I learned what it meant to live
as an adult in another culture,
to adapt to another way of being,
to burrow into a society that put
the group above the individual.

It was the year of vodka toasts,
acoustic guitar sing-a-longs over black bread
and summer-garden preserves,

of strolls along the pedestrian street
from Gorky Park to Menin Square,
along Bolshaya Pokrovskaya,

of craft beer purchased and carried away
in glass jugs we brought in ourselves,

strolls along the Volga River,
dollar tickets to operas and ballets and concerts.

What a monumental year, 1994—
the year we embraced and consumed life
like guests at a feast day table,
content but never ceasing to take more.

In 1994, we knew what it meant to live,
we knew what was important,
what we were destined to do
with our days, hours, minutes, seconds.

To think: during the same time
I was flying back to you,

others, elsewhere, were sitting at their desks,
debating decision memos,
barely living if living at all.

I feel sorry for those poor saps
who did not know how 1994 was supposed to be spent,

and wonder—for the thousandth time—

why we continue to put paycheck
ahead of what we know it means to live:

holding hands on a hillside,
blanket spread beneath us on the grassy bank,
sipping Soviet Champagne beside the shimmering, sunlit Volga.

We No Longer Kill Our Visitors

The millipede scurrying across the basement floor
searching for a dark corner in which to rest.

The spider dangling from the bottom of the bathroom windowsill,
working less enthusiastically as hot steam fills the room.

The stink bug rummaging over an orchid in the bay window,
not putting off any particular smell.

The mouse who found a bit of coffee cake on the kitchen floor,
darting back beneath the oven.

The bird who came in through the sliding door,
flying from room to room before finding an exit
through the open window.

The fruit bat spinning rings around each bedroom
before escaping through the attic vent.

These are our COVID guests,
our pandemic partners.

We don't retreat to the hardware store
in search of ways to trap or kill them.

We invite them in for a visit, a bit of dialogue—
wink of eye, twitch of nose—
and ask them not to be strangers
as they hide from us in the shadows
of our shared home.

steamy web

good morning
I say to the one who
shares my shower, but
before I can
touch her, or
ask her how long she
plans to stay, she has
already slipped
down the drain

Sacrifice for Sleep

"If I could only sleep till 9,"
she moans as she sits up
and falls back into bed,
bent over him like a hibiscus grown too tall.

"Saturday," he assures.
"You can sleep in on Saturday."

Saturday is five miles away,
each mile filled with a workday,

and when the weekend arrives
the work does not end.

The baby cries,
family stomachs growl,
playroom cluttered,
kitchen a mess,
friends call for counseling,
her man longs for her touch.

Once again,
she substitutes sacrifice
for sleep.

This Moment

As we sit at home—
me reading, you painting—
I remember

walking with you
on the cobblestoned hills of Lisbon's Alfama,
and boating across Lake Bled to ring
a Slovakian bell. I remember

ascending the Eiffel Tower, descending
into the Czech silver mines of Kutna Hora,
and soaking in a chrome tub full of hot,
hoppy beer in Chodova Plana.

My book has found its way to my lap
as I watch you put the finishing touches
on a watercolor. I remember

our children roaming Rome with us
and eating cream cake in Ljubljana;
exploring the Forbidden City in Beijing
and chasing bubbles during a jazz concert
in Krakow's Old Town Square.

So many perfect moments for scrapbook,
storybook memories.

You look up from your painting and smile,
the sound of the children's laughter
wafting up from the basement.

If I had to pick a perfect moment,
this moment
could very well be it.

Retirement Plans

Last week you announced your retirement,
talked about the traveling you planned to do at last,
lamenting that your mother had passed
and would not be traveling with you.

You had a spring in your step
as you anticipated the many exploratory steps to come.

You had begun to crack open the windows
and unlock the doors
to the private closets of yourself:
to share your poetry, your words
and insights, your heart and soul.

Those who knew you well
and those who knew you little agreed:
always a pleasure to run into you,
to have a few minutes of conversation
garnished with laughter and warmth.

Remember the retirement party
that even pandemic-work-at-home
social distance times could not dampen:

a hallway bursting at the rims
with friendly faces, asking your plans
for your first day of retirement,
where your travels will take you,
what sort of books you plan to read
or poems you plan to write.

Imagine heavy news on an overcast morning,
rainclouds barely managing to hold back droplets,
old friends and coworkers expressing sadness
at your one-day-prior-to-retirement-day passing.

And the joy,
if we can only look past our mourning,
to know that you got your initial wish:
traveling to an exciting new place,
exploring the unknown,
your mother at your side.

Dry Splash

All these years we've been worried about
the sea levels rising,
when what we should have paid attention to
was the fresh water levels falling.

Long-forgotten riverbeds and lake bottoms
reveal themselves
as dried mud,
cracked dirt,
rocks and sand.

The decades-long drought bears on,
waters evaporate,
the earth, dry.

I look into your moist eyes
and am reminded of the depths
beneath your surface,
the reserves hidden in those waters—
I want to dive in and
splash.

Last Call

We leaned on the bar,
barstools behind us,
conversed over martinis.

Dr. Griffith spoke of university days,
about our current work and families and lives,
and wondered where the time in between—
almost thirty years—
had gone.

My old professor's wife
chatted with a friend who happened by.

Our drinks were getting low when
Dr. Griffith excused himself for a moment.

I resolved then and there
to buy him a drink when he returned.

So many times I should have bought a drink,
deterred by the price, by time,
or by what may be misread.

A drink was long overdue.

When Dr. Griffith returned, he was distraught,
alarmed, frantic—I could see why.

His wife vanished—literally vaporized before our eyes—
her clothes still holding her form,
drifting slowly to the floor, a flat pile,
resembling the chalk outline of a body at a crime scene.

Dr. Griffith barely had the mind to say "fare thee well"
before he was swept away by medics and detectives.

As I watched him go
I realized I should not have waited for the right moment.
I should have bought him a drink when I had the chance.

I should have reached out to old friends, to new friends,
should have called more often,
should have written and emailed and texted.

The cast of my life, dear friends,
decades wedged between in-person visits.

I should have bought them all drinks, and often,
when I had the chance.

I resolved then and there,
as I ordered another martini,
that I should plan to attend the funeral—
and buy him a drink later,
when the time was right.

IV.

More (or Less)

Victimless

Sorting through relics in the attic,
I come across the dusty box,
wonder why I kept the evidence all these years.
I smile at the frightened adolescent I was.

I knew they were coming for me,
that it was only a matter of time
before an agent would reveal himself
from behind a tree, around a corner.

A man in a skinny tie on a park bench,
a woman in a dark pantsuit on the city bus,
even a sidewalk jogger with Walkman and headphones—
all potential apprehenders.

They knew what I'd done,
knew I'd been warned that my crime wasn't victimless.
No amount of feigning innocence
would lessen my prison sentence.

I have to laugh now, looking back,
as I open the box and peruse,
wonder where I can find an old VCR
for a glimpse of those jittery FBI warnings.

Poolside with Wilford Brimley

As a teenager, I remember watching *Cocoon,*
a movie about ancient men
searching for elusive youth.

My own children—now older than I was then—
sometimes watch classics with me,
immersing ourselves in another era.

A showering of alien cocoons
could not have taken me more by surprise
than when I learned Wilford Brimley
was only 49 years old when he played
that old, old man.

Have we discovered the fountain of youth
through medicine and science and healthy living,
me, two years older than that hoary Brimley,
yet still in a youngster's frame of mind?

Or is it that I think of the Wilford Brimley from *Cocoon*
and the Wilford Brimley selling diabetes medication on horseback
and the Wilford Brimley who eats oatmeal because
it's the right thing to do and the right way to do it
as one and the same?

This youth-centric movie
sends me peeking into neighborhood swimming pools
in search of an inviting glow.

Buried Reason

As I walk through the graveyard,
see the rolling farmland on hills beyond,
I think of the native Americans
who planted dead fish with their corn kernels

to fertilize and nurture,
to create life out of death,

and I see that the burying of the dead,
of those we love, did not begin
as a ritual of respect
or a suffocation of spreadable disease,

but as a *story*

intended to convince people who may not understand
why they really need to bury their dead—

to fertilize the earth.

Pests

In the cubed wastelands of the office,
an indoor ghost town,
tumbleweeds collect under plywood desks,
against felt walls and corners,
no open space to roam.

Mouse's homeland is abundant
with abandoned foods:

cookies and crackers, trail mix and packaged pies
all left behind, well preserved, easy to access—

a paradise of plenty, six square meals a day—
no predators.

The pandemic wears on,
food becomes harder to find,
and, once found, is barely palatable.

The distant companion at cube 3416 WHR
looks weak, too weak to put up a fight,
still enough meat on the bones,
at least at the moment.

It's an option, these final crumbs consumed.

People gradually return to their cubes,
not as often as before, only occasionally,
half a dozen sunrises and sunsets between intrusions.

Pizza crusts, crackers, cookies, crumbs:
scarce, but replenished.

Mouse's distant companion
never looked so relieved.

Thanks for the Socks

Thank you for the Christmas gift of socks,
immortalized in a photograph
collecting dust in an attic box.

You drove to the mall in your sable,
parked in the garage so you
wouldn't need to bear the snow.

That cozy evening beside the colorful, lit tree,
I presented you the harvest of heartache:
a book of cathartic poetry dedicated to you.

You, in turn, presented me
with a pair of argyle socks,
a thin red line across the toes.

I declared devotion in verse,
painted your beauty in rhyme and tempo,
alliteration and angst.

You accented the men's hosiery
with a framed picture of you wearing them
to personalize the gift.

Half a life later,
I revisit that poetry—
cringingly sincere, earnest, naïve—

and I wonder whether you still have a copy
reminding you that such worship as this
once put you at its center,

or whether your copy has been discarded
like the picture of an old acquaintance
or a worn-out pair of socks.

Elastic

Time is relative,
cannot be accurately measured.

Intervals are liquid, but not level,
minutes and hours not counted out
in quarts or gallons, miles or meters,
periods not sharing equal measure
on the space-time continuum.

Heavy moments fill space while others compress
into forgotten corners: buying groceries,
shopping for the fifth car (or was it the sixth?),
cursing out the insurance company,
writing another letter of complaint
or, occasionally, of praise.

But there are the trips to Europe,
the marvel of the Vatican and Saint Chapelle,
St. Basil's Cathedral and the Sagrada Familia,
and there were the Sawtooth Mountains and bluegrass,
the Grand Canyon and Niagara Falls,

and the phone calls that a grandparent died,
one by one, or a parent, a high school friend or co-worker,
the news of bad health and the treatment
to prolong but not cure.

Moments are fluid, unstable,
train rides and road trips
with long Kansas-crossing days that drag on
and exhilarating New-York-City-light nights
that zip by in a blink.

Layover

The Soviet-era airport:
a picture right out of my 1990s snapshots—
dark, dreary, harsh—
only this time without the machine-gunned guards
at passport control.

Time and time again, I went to the gate
to make sure I didn't miss the plane.

In the ceramic washroom, I found Sergey:
an old friend from my college stint in Russia.

He didn't know me at first,
my COVID beard and mane still growing,
but recognition grew on his expression
like facial hair.

Then another old friend, Olga, joined us,
and the three of us reminisced about hanging out
in dormitory washrooms of 1994 Russia,
flicking off the ash of the Soviet regime.

At Duty-Free, I purchased a bottle of Russian cognac—
brandy if you want to be literal, despite the label's claim—
and we drank to Russian-American friendship,
as we had decades ago.

What a shame, I proclaimed,
that we ran into one another
on the day of my departure.

When my flight number was announced on the PA system,
I bolted—but the plane lifted without me.

Sergey and Olga invited me to join them at a bench,
hours before their departure,
an open bottle of vodka and dried fish between them.

That's the danger of nostalgia:
stuck in a memory;
missing the moment.

Clog

She lays on her horn until
she realizes it's an accident that's
wedged
its way into her path.

Lights flash an eerie
glow
over collided frames,
twisted metal,
shattered glass,
crystal pebbles
on dark asphalt.

An old man on the street cries
into his cell phone
as the siren of a fire engine
rockets
up from behind.

She turns down the radio
and curses the driver who
clogs
the ambulance's way.

It isn't until later, as she
creeps
slowly by,
head turned, that she glimpses
the marooned sneaker
in the road.

A shame, she thinks,
as she picks up speed,
turns up the radio,
and realizes she's going to be
late
for her PTA meeting.

Countryman

Here's the paradox:
when I remember Countryman,
the thing I think about most is
other people.

Is it because of his surname? Conjuring
an image of community?
Neighbors meeting at afternoon socials
to discuss music and books, art and politics?

Perhaps his career as a copy editor,
workdays focused on the work of others,
improving it, making other writers better.

Could it be all those photographs of him,
always with compadres,
arms draped over shoulders, around waists,
admiring smiles directed at him,
reflected back to those privileged by his company?

Or his time spent among friends,
lifting our gently troubled spirits, even as he
endured weeks in the hospital, dates with doctors,
situations that would likely render the less hearty of us
hermitlike?

No.

When I think of him, I think of other people
because *he* thought of other people.

He didn't often share his work at readings or events—
he asked us to share ours.

His talent most prevalent:
the ability to make us feel appreciated,
a Countryman lending his sympathetic ear.

Groundhogs Don't Chuck

On an early September morning
the groundhog leaves his burrow,
drawn by the sound of plucked strings.

Venturing into the grass
to nibble on clover and dandelion,
the groundhog looks around
as the people begin to cackle
at the sight of him.

Munching on a discarded apple core,
the groundhog tries to understand their laughter.

A man balancing a chucking round in his arms
drops his heavy load and calls out,
"How much wood would a woodchuck chuck
If a woodchuck could chuck wood?"

The woodchuck sits upright
at the disturbing eruption of hoots and hollers.

These brutish men, who find strength in belittling,
howl the language of muscle and insult,
tossing smaller rounds of tree his way,
like inedible treats.

The woodchuck has never chucked wood—
has no desire to begin—
and he waddles slowly away from the ruckus
for a nap back in the comfort of his cool burrow.

Eric D. Goodman

Submission to a Student Magazine
(from a writer who's burning out)

I know you
like I know the crow's feet by my eyes—

you with your geyser talent
spewing young faithful words
that burn.

Inspired lines cool off,
dry up,
soak into the earth of age and detachment.

It gets harder.
Not the writing—holding on to the belief
that your words matter
in a world with
one hundred thousand writers.

There used to be a show about old people
called *Thirtysomething.*
You're too young to remember it
but I can't get it out of my mind.

I attend the college reading
celebrating another literary journal
that has rejected me.

I try to mingle
but find apprehension in your eyes.
I'm out of place.

The young writer is suddenly not.

I shake your hand and want to cling to it,
to hold it until you understand,
until you can feel what I feel
and know what it means to be one in
one hundred thousand writers.

Rug Pull

He had faith in the project
but didn't know what the project did.

The fundamentals were strong,
though not clearly defined.

The interest rate was out of this world,
not to mention the referral program

and the social media community
buzzed with positivity.

But the project's white paper did not include
a timetable indicating when, exactly,
the rug would be pulled.

Hammer

The children are kept
in a concrete room—
hungry, emaciated, bony—
lined up at the center.

A uniform paces behind them,
sledgehammer in hand.

The kids stand wide-eyed,
no more than nine or ten,
waiting, wondering.

When the hammer cracks
the first boy's skull
he doesn't comprehend.

Eyes bulge; not pain
so much as shock.

The others don't turn to look
but they hear. They know.

No time to think about escape
or to figure out what is transpiring.

One by one, whack by whack,
blood spurts as the hammer comes again.

Once to the ribs,
then to the face,
again to the back of the head.

Slain, their bloodied faces still plead.

Concentrate on why
hideous things happen
every day, still today.

Driving from comfortable office
to cozy home
in heated-seat car,

contemplating which book
to slide from shelf for fireside reading,
whether to dine in or out,
whether to sip brandy or whiskey,

it hits:
no wonder it's so hard to concentrate
on why these atrocities happen—
there's a bloody sledgehammer in my hands.

Knights that Pass in the Ship

Two knights in shining armor
join together at a round table
centered in the ship's dining hall.

One sits with his back to the window,
facing the door, watching.
His years as a royal guard informed him
that one should always watch for
a dark knight approaching.

The other sits with his back to the door,
preferring the view of the riverside beyond,
believing that most who approach from behind
do so with good intentions.

Those who watch for danger
have the advantage if it hits;
those who live with their breast plate off,
heart exposed,
may one day be injured.

So be it.

The knights part as friends,
each understanding new perspectives,
each clinging to old convictions.

Dogwoods

You stand in the backyard,
a married couple,
side by side on a wedding cake
of grass-green frosting.

You're a limier green than the grass,
branching out across the lower sky,
your combined breadth greater than the height
of your thirty-foot trunks.

Your torsos stand twenty paces apart;
your branches interlace,
becoming fine lines as winter cracks,

skeletal tentacles twisting and bending,
providing paths for squirrels,
perches for migrating birds.

Some winter days find you
trying on a new coat of ice,
or a shawl of white dust.

In spring, your radiant green leaves
unfurl around you like a new fashion,
white flowers accessorizing.

In summer, those leaves become lush,
larger, darker, greener.

Lounge chairs find their way beneath your branches,
and books of fiction and poetry,
magazines and glasses of lemonade and pilsner.

The dog digs holes in your mulch pad,
keeping the deer and squirrels at bay.

As autumn extinguishes summer's warm breath
you bear large, red berries,
spotting your deep green coat,
like a holly-tree Halloween costume.

Squirrels find reason to visit your branches again
partaking in your harvest,

and deer creep from the surrounding woods
for a dessert of your low-hanging berries,

which fall as your leaves change shade,
leaf following berry,
until you are at your core once again:

two skeletons of twisting, bending branches
reaching across a bright, sunless sky
to touch one another,
console one another,
warm one another
in the cold.

Tremble

Remember
curiosity and exploration,
venturing to faraway lands and dark alleys
not knowing or fearing what we may find there—
yearning novelty,

going with the flow,
inquisitiveness guiding us,

being Bill Murray,
one day busting ghosts or gophers on screen,
the next, bussing tables or doing dishes
in the home of a college student,
striking up a conversation with a stranger at a dive bar,
then following them home to partake in the ongoing party.

Not the confirmed plans and stabilities of today,
dinners and outings like meetings in a busy workday.

Not the patio loungers of tomorrow,
birdsong in backyard as we read novels,
watch the dog chase a squirrel up the tree,
sigh, and think, *this is nice.*

Shall we trade in these securities,
seek out uncertainty,
not knowing what tomorrow will bring,

but waking, trembling,
daring to find out?

EPILOGUE

Taste

Water rolls in the kettle.

The spout's bird whistles
a call to action.

Across the counter,
you fill the cast-iron teapot
with a generous helping
of loose oolong tea.

Steeping fills the air
with earthy aroma.

Pour into a ceramic cup,
add a touch of honey.

You in chair,
cup in hand,
tea in cup,
all in place.

Snow falls in a gentle, rhythmic hush
beyond the picture window.

Just the right moment to taste.

AFTERWORD

Although I have written poetry before, I've been primarily a prose writer: fiction and creative non-fiction. As the pandemic found many of us shuttered up in our homes, I found myself drawn to poetry—reading it and writing it. It would seem that being home and no longer needing to commute would provide more time for long-form writing, but I felt as though I had less focus time during the pandemic than before. This is partially what attracted me to poetry.

Poetry seems a perfect form for today's society—short, concise, and able to get a point or feeling or idea across succinctly. That appealed to me as a reader, and especially as a writer. Rather than jot down and file away ideas that came to me for future stories, novels, or plot development, I was able to use them as the basis for poetry.

The pandemic was also a time to question life as we know it, to reminisce about life as we knew it, and to consider what life will be as we emerge back into a new normalcy. Poems proved an ideal vehicle for such a mood and frame of mind.

The result, for me, is my first collection of poetry—hopefully not my last. I have thoroughly enjoyed working on *Faraway Tables*.

I want to thank the poets and friends who gave me guidance, advice, and who provided kind criticism as I worked on fine-tuning these poems and this book: Shirley J. Brewer, Charles Rammelkamp, Nitin Jagdish, Sherry Audette Morrow, Sid Gold, and Toby Devens.

A shout-out to my family is in order. They not only came along for the ride—sometimes they probably felt like they were strapped in the back seat as I bulleted ahead into traffic at full throttle.

Appreciation to the editors of literary journals, magazines, and publications that are included in the Acknowledgement section, who shared individual poems from this collection with their readers.

Finally, my sincere thanks to Kent and Laura Denmark of Yorkshire Publishing for believing in this manuscript and taking a chance by publishing my first collection of poetry, to Mike Smith for his thoughtful edits and recommendations, and to Serena Hanson and her team for bringing the book to life.

ACKNOWLEDGEMENTS

The author and publisher gratefully acknowledge the editors who included these poems in the following publications.

"Patience" in *Main Street Rag*
"Water Fall Blues" in *Gargoyle Magazine*
"Embracing Hermithood" in *Gargoyle Magazine*
"Yin Yang Yankee Doodle" in *Loch Raven Review*
"Fado" in *Syncopation Literary Journal*
"Avocado Toast" in *Border Beats*
"Sisson's" in *North of Oxford*
"Fire Pit Season" in *North of Oxford*
"Hammer" in *North of Oxford*
"We No Longer Kill Our Visitors" in *North of Oxford*
"Just Enough" in *Syndic Literary Journal*
"Layover" in *Syndic Literary Journal*
"Last Call" in *Syndic Literary Journal*
"Moments" in *Syndic Literary Journal*
"Toast to Friendship" in *Syndic Literary Journal*
"Dry Splash" in *Bourgeon*
"Immersion" in *Bourgeon*
"Give Control" in *Bourgeon*
"Social Media Boycott" in *Mid-Atlantic Review*
"Sacrifice for Sleep" in *Mid-Atlantic Review*
"Of the Castle" in *Power of the Feminine*
"Rug Pull" in *Beatnik Cowboy*
"Gulp" in *The Five-Two*
"Victimless" in *The Five-Two*

Eric D. Goodman

"Knights That Pass in the Ship" in *The Fictional Café*
"Newsworthy" in *The Fictional Café*
"Buried Reason" in *The Fictional Café*
"Backyard Weeds" in *The Fictional Café*
"Power of Positive Thinking" in *Cajun Mutt Review*
"Celebratory Condolence" in *Bold Monkey Review*
"Barefoot" in *Bold Monkey Review*
"The Web in Your Path" in *Bold Monkey Review*
"Pests" in *Which Side are You On?*
"steamy web" in *Life in Me Like Grass on Fire*
"Relics" in *Blue Collar Review*
"Retirement Plans" in *Blue Collar Review*
"Countryman" in *The Three Acts of Wayne Countryman*
"Submission to a Student Magazine" in *Grub Street*
"Taste" in *Fleas on the Dog*
"Thanks for the Socks" in *Sparks of Calliope*
"As for the Ticket" in *BlazeVox*
"Tremble" in *BlazeVox*

ABOUT THE AUTHOR

Eric D. Goodman lives and writes in Maryland, where he remained sheltered in place with his family for most of the pandemic, spending a portion of his hermithood writing poetry.

He's author of six previously published books of fiction, including *Wrecks and Ruins* (Loyola University's Apprentice House Press, 2022) *The Color of Jadeite* (Apprentice House, 2020), *Setting the Family Free* (Apprentice House, 2019), *Womb: a novel in utero* (Merge Publishing, 2017), *Tracks: A Novel in Stories* (Atticus Books, 2011), and *Flightless Goose*, (Writers Lair Books, 2008).

More than a hundred short stories, articles, and travel stories have been published in literary journals, magazines, and periodicals.

Eric's recent poems have been featured in more than twenty publications, including *Gargoyle Magazine*, *The Main Street Rag*, *Blue Collar Review*, *Loch Raven Review*, *Syndic Literary Journal*, *Fictional Café*, *The Five-Two*, *Mid-Atlantic Review*, *North of Oxford*, and others.

Eric is co-creator and curator of the Lit & Art Reading Series, Baltimore's longest-running literary series, and a prose and poetry editor at *BrickHouse Books*, Maryland's oldest small press.

Learn more about Eric and his writing at www.EricDGoodman.com.